To: Sis Margo

The phrase is often used "We would rather see a sermon than hear one" Thank you for the sermon you preach every day.

love you

T. Harrison

Thou <u>SHALT</u> be Saved...

God's biblical plan of salvation for your life

BY

TWYLA D. HARRISON

authorHOUSE™

1663 LIBERTY DRIVE, SUITE 200
BLOOMINGTON, INDIANA 47403
(800) 839-8640
WWW.AUTHORHOUSE.COM

First published by AuthorHouse 06/06/05

ISBN: 1-4208-4914-X (sc)

Printed in the United States of America
Bloomington, Indiana

This book is printed on acid-free paper.

All scriptures quoted are taken from the King James Version of the Holy Bible unless otherwise noted.

DEDICATION PAGE

First and foremost I want to thank my Lord and Savior Jesus Christ. Without him I would be and am nothing! To the four reasons I get up each morning, my babies, G'anecia, D'Quynton, Carlesia & Kyla. I believe God to do great things in your lives. I stand on God's word that if I train you up in the way you should go when you get old you won't depart from it. I've tried to give you the most important and valuable thing you will ever posses, Jesus. Always remember that no matter where you may find yourself in life never forget God. He is the only one that can forgive, heal and save. I want to give honor and reverence to the one God used to bring me into this world, my mother, Pamela Wells of Muskogee, Oklahoma. To the parents that raised me in the fear and admonition of the lord, my grandparents, Pastor Florean Wright and the late Eugene Wright both of Muskogee, Oklahoma. To my god-mother and aunt, Betty Willis of Muskogee, Oklahoma who has always taught me to reach for the very best that is within me and never stop until I succeed. To the ones who gave me my start in the ministry, Prophetess Ola Mae Washington, Pastor of Jubilee Evangelistic Outreach Ministries of Beaufort, South Carolina along with Pastor A.H. and Marlene Jones, Pastors of Old Agency Baptist Church of Muskogee, Oklahoma. To my dear

Pastor, Apostle and elect lady Marnita Archie of Faith Deliverance Christian Center in Muskogee, Oklahoma. I appreciate God so much for the both of you. You two have really proven to be a true man and woman of God. Thank you for seeing the God in me and never failing to remind me that I can do all things through Christ that strengthens me. Elect lady Marnita, thank you for teaching me to never hang my head down because of what I have encountered in this life because everything I've gone through has truly made me what I am today. To two very dear friends of mine, Ms.Marilyn Frazier of Beaufort South Carolina, believe it or not you encourage me as much as I do you. Mrs. Melita McCoy, you came to my rescue when I thought all hope for me was gone. You have truly been an Elizabeth to me. You will always have a special place in my heart. To the former Victorious Women group Muskogee division. To a very special brother, Byron Warner and family of Muskogee, Oklahoma. I love you guy's sooo much! Stay strong in the lord always. The lord has an awesome work for both you and your family. To every well-wisher and to every enemy. Without any enemies there can be no table spread. God has promised that he would prepare a table before me in the presence of my enemies so thank you all. God is truly building his church and the gates of hell will not prevail against it. I love you all.

TABLE OF CONTENTS

INTRODUCTION

This book is accredited to the one who has given me life and that more abundantly, my Lord and Savior Jesus Christ. I pray that this book will be an inspiration to all that seek a greater walk with God. My prayer is that every word read will be used as a seed in your life to bring forth an abundant harvest. This book is not designed in any way to condemn anyone nor their beliefs. What it is designed to do is awake every believer who has confessed Jesus Christ as their lord and are awaiting his soon return to a higher level of "holiness" in their Christian walk. May God continue to allow his anointing to rest upon his people. Be encouraged in the lord always.

With the love of the lord,
The Author

CHAPTER ONE

"Confession is only the beginning"

WHAT IT MEANS TO BE SAVED

Throughout the years the word "saved" has been misused, misunderstood and sadly to say abused. When the question is posed, are you saved? The response echoes "what do you mean by saved? Do I believe in God? Yeah". Too many people that phrase (are you saved) is interpreted many different ways. To a churchgoer it may mean I'm faithful in church attendance or that I've joined a church or even that I've been baptized. To a non-church goer it may mean I don't go to church but I consider myself a good person. To a backslider it may mean I use to go to church and now I don't so their response may be I used to be. Whatever category you may fall in the main issue is that we need to and must settle biblically what it really means to be saved.

Because of a lack of understanding of Romans 10:8-10 everyone that has ever acknowledged verbally that there is a God or anyone that has experienced a background in a church setting declares to be saved regardless of the lifestyle they may be leading. There are some that will adamantly declare that they are "saved" and all the while they have a joint in their pocket, a liquor bottle in their hand and their live-in lover waiting for them at the house. In the society we live in today, we have men and women being ordained as ministers of the gospel with their homosexual or lesbian lover by their side. Something is drastically wrong with this picture. In addition to all of these outward displays, there are those that have never confessed Jesus as Lord yet they contend that heaven is theirs simply because they are a "good" person. This to is a great deception in the world today. "Neither is there salvation in any other: for there is none other name under heaven given among men, whereby we must be saved" Acts 4:12. Jesus' work of the cross is what gives us access into the Holy place (heaven) therefore a confession of Christ is in fact the first prerequisite for salvation, not just being a "good" person. After careful study of God's word I've come to realize that a daily confession that one is saved really means that you have confessed Jesus Christ as lord of your life, accepted and received him into your heart and are now running the Christian race by faith. It means you have forgotten the things behind you and you are now pressing towards the mark of the prize of the high calling of God in Christ Jesus.

To confess you are saved means you have separated yourself from the lifestyle of the world and are no longer entangled with the bondage of sin. We who confess salvation believe, by faith, that our eternal future is secure with God according to the word he has given us. I pray that by the time you reach the end of this book you will have a greater understanding of God's plan of salvation for your life.

ENTERING THE RACE

Several times in scripture the Christian race is paralleled to a race. Ecc.9: 11 states that the race is not given to the swift nor the battle to the strong. I Cor. 9:24 goes on to say *"know ye not that they which run in a race run all, but one recieveth the prize? So run that ye may obtain"*. Notice that Paul doesn't focus so much on how many entered or started the race but his emphasis was on the one who finished—endured to the end.

As a follower of Christ the prize we desire to obtain is eternal life with our Savior, that is, Jesus Christ himself (Romans 6:23). As one who has been redeemed from the grip and law of sin and death our greatest desire should be to lay eyes on, be in the presence of and behold face to face, Jesus himself. The one who bore our sickness, carried our grief's, purchased us back from hell's hold, forgave us of all unrighteousness and placed us in right standing with God our Father.

Everyone would love to believe that his or her life would end in total bliss. We would all love to believe that after a wearied life of sacrifice to our families, dedication to a local assembly and many countless charitable acts that our reward would be eternal life in the presence of God almighty. However, scripture is clear in expressing two very serious points, one being that in latter times some shall depart from the faith (I Tim. 4:1). Many people interpret this to mean that there will be a great falling away of church attendance but bible readers understand that when the word faith is used in describing a group of people it's referring to the body of believers, God's glorious church. Paul admonishes us in Gal. 6: 10 to do good to everyone especially to them who are of the household of "faith". In order to depart from something means you had to first be a part of it. So according to Paul there will be some who will confess with their mouth that God raised Jesus from the dead and say that they believe in their heart as well. They will enter the race but this group of people will not finish their course but will leave or depart from the body of believers.

So what now? Is confession alone enough to secure eternal salvation? According to the word of God, every knee shall bow and every tongue will confess (Romans 14:11) but not every one will enter the kingdom of heaven. James 2:19 NLT says, "Do you still think it's enough just to believe that there is one God? Well, even the demons believe this, and they tremble in terror!" Matthew agrees by recording in Matt. 7:21 "Not everyone that saith unto me, lord, lord shall enter into the kingdom of heaven; but he that doeth the will of my father which is in heaven". Confession is only the beginning!

Point two of what scripture is clear in expressing is that only those that endure to the end shall be saved (Matt.24: 13). Remember Paul said everyone in a race is running but only the one who finishes will receive the prize. Notice the word shall in both Matt 24:13 and Rom. 10:9. Many time the word of God is quoted to mean that if you confess with your mouth the lord Jesus and believe in your heart that God raised him from the dead then you ARE saved and that is clearly a misquote of the scripture. The word shall stems from the word will, which means something that is going to eventually happen. If you confess and believe, you will eventually be saved! When? Once you've endured to the end. Confession is only the beginning. Confessing Christ as Lord and Savior means you have now entered the race (the Christian walk) but the race you've now entered must be finished. Of course now that you've confessed Jesus as lord and have made a declaration to run the Christian race, you speak those things that be not as though they were. Just as we boldly confess that we are rich and don't have a dime in our pocket. Just as we boldly confess

7

that we are healed when often times our bodies are racking with pain. Just as we boldly confess that we are strong when we don't feel one ounce of strength. So also we speak a daily confession of "I'm saved" because that's our desired end. Faith cometh by hearing! The dilemma that we are faced with today is that many people believe that since a confession has been made that they are guaranteed eternal life despite the lifestyle they lead thereafter. They will go so far as to say that the blood of Jesus covers their sinful lifestyle but Hebrews 10:26 NLT clearly records " Dear friends, if we deliberately continue sinning after we have received a full knowledge of the truth, there is no other sacrifice that will cover these sins". In fact in that same passage of scripture it tells us that there will be nothing to look forward to but the terrible expectation of God's judgment and the raging fire that will consume his enemies. Paul goes on to say in Hebrew 5:9 that Jesus became the author of eternal salvation to them that obey. I Peter 4:17 reminds us that judgment is going to begin at the house of God but then he asks if it first begins with us, what shall the end be of them that obey not the gospel of God? Verse 18 NLT (same book and chapter) " If the righteous are barely saved, what chance will the godless and sinner have?" Notice the three different groups of people Paul addressed.

The righteous, those who confessed Jesus as Lord and maintained holiness. The ungodly, those who confessed Jesus but continued to sin after the flesh. The sinner, those who never confessed Jesus at all.

Scripture admonishes us to be steadfast, unmovable, always abounding in the work of the lord (I Cor. 15:58). It instructs us to continue rooted and grounded in the word and to finish our course. Paul says it like this in II Tim. 4:7, 8 NLT *"I have fought a good fight, I have finished the race and I have remained faithful. And now the prize awaits me—the crown of righteousness that the lord, the righteous judge will give me on that great day of his return"*. It was only after Paul's race had been completed that he received "the prize". No runner in a marathon, any NBA teams any NFL teams or a pageant contestant etc. Will ever be given a prize, an award, recognition or special honors halfway through the respectful event. It is only after all requirements have been met, the finish line has been crossed and endurance has been displayed that they will receive what they've worked so hard to obtain...the prize.

SHALL...

Just for a moment lets look at several scriptures that reflect a future expectation in response to the word shall. Gen. 2: 17 records instructions given to humanity concerning their occupancy in the Garden of Eden. It states *"But of the tree of the knowledge of good and evil, thou shalt not eat of it: for in the day that thou eatest thereof thou shalt surely die"*. As previously stated, shall points to something that will transpire. The word "shall" indicates process. Since humanity was created to live forever, Adam and eve's rebellion brought death (separation from God) upon all humanity while setting in course the dying process. Notice that when they sinned no physical manifestation was seen. It wasn't until 930 years later that the promise God had made would physically come to pass. Adam was 930 years old before his physical body died (Gen. 5:5) interesting huh? Look if you will at some other promises that transpired over a period of time.

Abraham, the father of faith, when he received the word from God that his seed would be more than the number of stars in the sky (Gen.15: 5) had no manifestation at all of a son. Let's continue. Abram was the name that denoted his fleshly nature while Abraham was the name that denoted his spiritual nature. Keep in mind that flesh will always go against the will of God. Gen. 15:6 says that Abram (the flesh) believed in the lord (and that seems to be the argument of most people today "I believe in the lord" but once again, lets continue). For a moment, lets look at what transpired in the time frame of when he was Abram to when he became Abraham. Abram received the word spoken over his life by the lord but for a season, operated in his flesh. Before Abram could move into the thing that God had spoken over his life, it was a must that he repent (rethink his position and turn from the flesh) and come into covenant with God. A covenant is a binding agreement between two or more people to do or not to do something. The covenant between God and Abram was this, Gen. 17:1, 2 Walk before me and be thou perfect. And I will... Abram then fell on his face and talked with God and it was then that God reaffirmed the promise already made to him. God now changes his name from Abram to Abraham symbolizing the covenant made between Abram and himself (Gen. 17:5). God promised Abram saying look now towards heaven, and tell the stars, if thou be able to number them: and he said unto him, so <u>shall</u> thy seed be. Did Abram instantly have that many descendants? No. It wasn't until Abraham was 99 years old that the promised seed manifested. Abraham <u>eventually</u> became the father of many nations.

Just as a reference, lets continue on in the lineage of Abraham. Jacob was a man born into the lineage of an already spoken promise. Jacob was the grandson of Abraham. God, as previously covered, promised to bless the nations through the seed of Abraham. In the 32nd chapter of Genesis we see the wrestling of Jacob with a man. This wrestle transpired for the sole purpose of transforming Jacob (the flesh) into Israel (the spirit). Those familiar with the story of Jacob know that he was a man of great deceit and trickery. He was a trickster and labeled at birth as a heel grabber. In Jacob's lifetime he tricked his brother into selling or giving over his birthright for a piece of bread and pottage of lentiles (Gen.25: 29-4). He deceived his father into believing that he was in fact his elder brother thus receiving the blessing of the first-born son (Gen.27: 1-29). Jacob was very fleshly and that's exactly how he operated. The flesh will always do whatever it has to do to gratify itself. But Jacob was faced with a very serious problem; he was to be heir of his grandfather, Abraham. God could not and would not intrust Jacob with the kingdom (his authority, power and glory) while living and operating in the flesh.

Real quick, lets back up to Gen. 32:22-29. Here we see a conversation between Jacob and the man he wrestled with. Jacob was being confronted about his fleshly nature. During this wrestle, Jacob would not release the man until he blessed him. By admitting whom he was opened the door for him to receive the blessing he wrestled so hard to obtain. What I thought to be interesting in this story is although the promise of a name and nature change was spoken and released in verse 28 of chapter 32, Jacob's name did not manifest immediately. The very next chapter begins by saying *"And Jacob lifted up his eyes, and looked..."* Chapter 34:5 states *"And Jacob heard..."* Chapter 35:1 begins by saying *"And God said unto Jacob..."* In verses 9&10 of chapter 35 God returns to Jacob to reaffirm and establish what had been promised earlier, just as he did with Abraham. At this point Jacob has repented and put away all other gods that had been before him and his family (Gen.35: 2-7). Jacob cleansed himself and sacrificed to God, which put him in position to receive God's promise. It wasn't until verse 21 of chapter 35 that Israel was manifested. Jacob eventually became Israel after repentance, sacrifice and great endurance.

So far we've talked about two men that received a word from God and followed his plan to receive what was theirs. Now look at two more men that received words from God but didn't receive what God had for them. Moses was a man chosen by God to lead his people out of bondage and into the Promised Land (exodus 3:10) but because of disobedience he was not allowed into the land God ultimately wanted him to enter (numbers 20:12).

Moses was a man used by God to perform many signs and wonders in the sight of God's people (Exodus 7:8-12, 7:15-20, 8:5-13, 8:16-19, 8:20-26) but despite the forty years of dedication to the voice of God one disobedient act would change his destiny forever. God demands total obedience. He is very clear in expressing that obedience brings blessings and disobedience brings cursings (Deuteronomy 28:2, 15). One other man hand picked by Jesus to be his follower was Judas Iscariot. This man, as mentioned, was chosen and called out by Jesus himself (Luke 6:16). Notice closely that in Luke 6, Jesus called his disciple to him and of them he chose twelve, which he named apostles (Luke 6:13). So you mean to tell me that Judas, the one that would betray the Son of God, was an apostle? Not only was he an apostle but he also, along with the other disciples, preformed many miracles and signs and wonders (Luke 10:17-20, Acts 14:3 NLT). So what went wrong with Judas? Well the word of God tells us to guard our hearts for out of it flow the issues of life. It also goes on to say that lust when it is finished bringeth forth sin and sin when it is finished bringeth forth death (James 1:15). The whole point is that just because you start out walking with God does not guarantee you will finish with him. Confession is only the beginning. Judas was faithful to the call of Jesus, <u>for a season</u>.

There were many that started out with Jesus but did not continue on with him. The question is will you leave the one you confessed as lord or will you finish what you've started?

Jesus, the savior of the world, was given to die for the sins of the world. His mother, Mary, was given specific instructions concerning the conception, birth and future name of the child she would carry. The angel instructed Mary to name the child Jesus for he <u>shall</u> save his people from their sins (Matt. 1:21). Because God's laws and principles never change Jesus himself would also have to display great endurance as well as finish his course. Jesus was made a man. He was flesh therefore he experienced the same things we experience. He was tempted in all points just as we are yet was he without sin (Hebrews 4:15). Jesus endured great tribulation just as we must. He was faithful to the work the father gave him. Even Jesus himself was not excluded from the law and principles of God the father. He had to lead a holy life (I peter 1:16) and he had to finish his course by enduring to the end (John 17:4 & 19:30). The mere fact that Jesus was born did not save humanity from their sins but the fact that he finished what he was sent to do. It was 33 years between the time that the angel told Mary her child would save his people from their sins to when redemption was actually manifest. Jesus <u>eventually</u> saved his people from their sins.

If God's law did not change even for his very own son, there is no way we can think that it will change for us. Am I saying that you can't be confident in your salvation? Absolutely not! What am I saying? I'm saying that a confession of Jesus does not give you liberty to continue in sin. There is no way we can lead a life of iniquity and declare that eternal life is ours simply because at one point in our lives we made a verbal confession! The word declares that if you <u>continue</u> in my word, <u>then</u> are ye my disciples in deed (John 8:31). The statement "if you continue" indicates that at some point there was an entrance or beginning in God's word (or in him, for he is his word). God, through his word, shows us in Hebrews 6:4-6 that it is possible for one to receive him, walk with him, take part in the benefits of God and then fall away. I pray that by now you at least see a pattern that must be followed.

The word of God is a guide that tells you how to overcome every obstacle that may occur while running your race (II Peter 1:3)

Confession is only the beginning; you've now entered the race so run that ye may obtain. Romans chapter 13 admonishes us to remain in submission and obedience in accordance to God's greatest commandment, which is love, for now is our salvation nearer than when we believed. The NLT says it this way in Romans 13:11 *"Another reason for right living is that you know how late it is; time is running out. Wake up, for the coming of our salvation is nearer than when we first believed"*.

Hmm, this poses a very interesting point. If in fact confession of Jesus alone guarantees we already possess or have salvation why does scripture declare that our salvation is soon to come? Remember saints; we are saved by grace through Faith. *"What is faith? It is the confident assurance that what we hope for is going to happen. It is the evidence of things we cannot yet see"* (Hebrews 11:1NLT). Faith is the hope we cling to until there is a manifestation. Romans 8:23, 24 says *"We are saved by hope: but hope that is seen is not hope: for what a man seeth, why doth he yet hope for it? But if we hope for that we see not, then do we with patience wait for it"*. In other words if you already have something why are you hoping for it? Since hope is such a significant part of faith I decided to look up the word hope. Webster's New World Thesaurus defines hope as …**Hope** *n*.1. [Reliance upon the future], faith, expectation, wish, goal, dream. It also defines it as…**Hope** *v*. wish, desire, look forward to, await, dream, watch for, be prepared for, make plans for. (Both definitions are partially quoted). We walk or live by faith so in turn we walk or live in the expectancy of salvation, we are hoping for salvation. *"And do not bring sorrow to the Holy Spirit by the way you live. Remember, he is the one who has identified you as his own, guaranteeing that you will be saved on the day of redemption"* Ephesians 4:30 NLT. Hebrews 9:28 NLT says, *" so also Christ died only once as a sacrifice to take away the sins of many people. He will come again but not to deal with our sins again. This time he will bring salvation to all those who are eagerly waiting for him"*.

God has given us a blue print for salvation and our faith and confession must line up with that blue print, his written word. Many people feel that faith is simply positive confessions. "I believe in God, so I'm saved", that's positive confession. "Because I've confessed Jesus as lord, believe in my heart and accepted the work of the cross and am maintaining holiness, I'm saved". That's faith! Romans 13:11 brought out a very significant step in the plan of salvation. It stated, another reason for right living… well, scripture says that without holiness (right living) no man shall see God (Hebrew 12:14). So you can confess day and night that you are heaven bound but if your life is full of iniquity (sin) your confession is null and void. It wouldn't make much sense for me to go out and buy a cookbook, read it, study it and declare that I'm going to make a cherry pie. But when it's time for me to purchase the ingredients what I get is: eggs, oil, flour, baking powder, sugar, butter and maybe some icing and the whole time I'm still saying "I'm gonna make a cherry pie. I read the book and understand it so I believe with all my heart I'm going to have a cherry pie". Everyone that knows how to cook knows that this is not the recipe for cherry pie. Most importantly the main ingredient wasn't even mentioned...cherries! How does that sound? A little off huh? Well it's the same in our daily life. We have people everyday declaring something that is totally contrary to the recipe of salvation, which is the written word of God. They've contributed a lot of things in their life, giving to the poor, feeding the hungry and church attendance but the main ingredient is missing... holiness. II Tim.2: 19 NLT records *"But God's truth stands firm like a foundation stone with this inscription: The lord knows those that are his and those who claim they belong to the lord <u>must</u> turn away from all wickedness"*. Holiness is a vital step in salvation. Without it no man (human) will see God.

CHAPTER TWO

"Go beyond the starting line, launch out into the deep"

WHAT NEXT?

At this point someone may be asking okay, I've confessed with my mouth and I believe in my heart that God raised Jesus from the dead— I've entered the race—what next? Well the word of God says in Hebrew 12:1 NLT. *"Therefore, since we are surrounded by such a huge crowd of witnesses to the life of faith, let us strip off every sin that so easily hinders our progress, And let us run with endurance the race that God has set before us"*. Now that we've entered the Christian race we must begin to lay aside the weights and sins that would hinder our progress. Because sin separates you from God and your desire now is to be close to him, you begin to remove the sin in your life that will keep you from your newly confessed Savior. The word that stuck out the most to me was the word endurance! This to is a vital step in the plan of salvation. Remember only the one who endures to the end SHALL be saved. Luke 8:11-15 gives an example of some that entered the race but did not go on to complete it. Here we see four groups of people that all received the same seed (the word of God) but had very different outcomes. The illustration I want to deal with is the seed that fell on the rocky path (Luke 8:13, Matt. 13:20-21, Mark 4:

16-17) or a stony heart. This person received the word they heard with joy and believed <u>for a while</u> but because the word they received had no root, in the time of temptation they fell away. Faith comes by hearing and hearing by the word of God (Romans 10:17). Now that you've entered the race you must begin to lay aside the weights and sins that would hinder your walk with God. In addition you must begin to feed yourself the word of God for it is in God's word that you will find life. This group of people fell away because they had a lack of faith or lack of the word.

Faith is the attribute that will cause you to endure to the end. It is also the attribute that will cause you to become a Son of God and not just a child of God. The word says in John 1:12, that to all whom <u>received</u> him (that's where you are when you enter the race, the place of receiving) to them gave he power to become the Sons of God. Once you receive Christ you now have the ability or the power to go forward in God. The seed you receive must not lay dormant in your life but rather it must be watered, by the word, so that it can develop and come forth. The word sons denote identity. It means you've moved from just receiving Christ into your heart and acknowledging that he is lord to actually being born, birth or adopted into the family of God

(Refer to Romans 8:15, Galatians 4:5, Ephesians 1:5). According to John 3:3-7 without this birth you cannot see nor enter the kingdom of God. As stated, faith is the element that will usher you into this birth. It is faith by and through the Holy Spirit that gives you power to become. Everyone that receives Christ, he is given a measure of faith (Romans 12:3). Now you must allow the Holy Spirit, which is the power of God, to take you from faith to faith (Romans 1:17). Paul tells us in I Peter 1:5 that our spiritual preservation or our level of endurance depends on "the power of God through our faith". But we must not stop at just having faith; we must develop and add to our faith. II Peter 1:5 says to add to your faith virtue; and to virtue knowledge; and to knowledge temperance; and to temperance patience; and to patience godliness; and to godliness brotherly kindness; and to brotherly kindness charity. Verse 8 of the NLT reads, *"The more you grow like this, the more you will become productive and useful in your knowledge of our lord Jesus Christ"*. Colossians 2:6, 7 NLT says it this way, *"And now, just as you accepted Christ Jesus as your Lord, you must continue to live in obedience to him. Let your roots grow down into him and draw up nourishment from him, so you will grow in faith, strong and vigorous in the truth you were taught"*. In other words if you follow this pattern you will develop roots in the word of God that will cause you to endure and not to fall away.

The question was posed what next? Well, after you receive Jesus into your heart you must go on to be born again. What does that mean? It means you must move from just acknowledging Jesus as lord to actually displaying the characteristics of the Christ nature. As you continue in Christ you will eventually come to a place in your life where you leave the sins of the flesh, producing holiness, God's nature. We are to become exactly who God is, for we were created in his very image (Gen.1: 26) and we were predestined to be conformed into his reflection (Romans 8:29). We are to talk as he talked, walk as he walked, think as he thought and live as he lived (I John 2:6). Many people argue that Jesus was able to live the life he did because he was literally God in the flesh and that is true BUT...aren't we? I John 4:17 says, *"Herein is our love made perfect that we may have boldness in the Day of Judgment: because as he is, so are we in this world"*. John 10:34 continues by saying *"Jesus answered them, Is it not written in your law, I said, ye are gods?"* If that isn't enough, psalm 82:6 says, *"I have said, ye are gods; and all of you are children of the most High".* To often excuses are made as to why we (humanity) cannot live the holy life God has called us to. God would never command us to do something that he knew we could not attain to and he does command holiness from those professing him as Savior and Lord. We must come to a place in God where we become the very essence of who he is and that is HOLY. The bottom line is, the same thing that dwelled within Jesus is the same thing that dwells in us, the Spirit of God. Greater is he that is in us than he that is in the world. (I John 4:4)

COMING INTO

Behold, I stand at the door, and knock: If any man hear my voice, and open the door, I will come in to him, and will sup with him, and he with me.

Revelations 3:20

When you receive Jesus into your heart, there is a three-fold effect that takes place. Jesus, who is in the father, is now in you and you in him (John 14:20). Now the spirit that you've yielded to must lead you in every endeavor of your life. It is when you allow the Spirit of God to lead you that proves you are a Son of God according to

Romans 8:14. If indeed the Spirit of God dwells in you then you no longer operate from the realm of the flesh but from the realm of the spirit. If the Spirit of God does not control, lead and guide you then you are none of his (Romans 8:9). After this three-fold effect takes place you now have access into the holy of holies. You now have the power to operate beyond the flesh (Hebrews 10:19, 20) and to begin to be governed by the Spirit thus producing holiness, the very essence of who God is. In the natural, when a man and a woman want to have a baby, the seed giver, the man, deposits something inside the woman with the expectation that what he put inside of her will form and eventually be birthed. No woman stays pregnant forever. When she receives seed from her husband her body immediately begins to change. Some days she feels good some days she feels bad. I would parallel this to the times in life that we fall. In the midst of all the things the woman goes through in this season of her life there comes a time when a birthing takes place. What is it really that a man wants to see? Any real man wants to see himself. It gives him a great sense of pride to hear someone say "boy you sure look like your daddy" or "you act just like your daddy". Well, I believe it is the same way with God. He has put his precious seed inside of humanity, with the expectation that the seed will form and be birthed (Galatians 4:19). God desires to see himself, his nature and his character. According to I John 3:8-10 NLT the manifestation of who your father is comes from the conduct you display. We love to talk about the process but when are God's people going to come to a place of birthing? Does your conduct reflect the nature and character of the Heavenly Father?

HOW DO I DIE?

I protest by your rejoicing, which I have in Christ Jesus our Lord, I die daily.

I Corinthians 15:31

In order for something to live something must die! For this very reason did Jesus, the Savior of the world, die for humanity (John11: 50, 18:14). Under the law and rule of the old covenants, people would kill and sacrifice diverse kinds of animals in order to cover their sins allowing them to live. Study: Leviticus 1:1-7, 2:1-16, 3:1-7, 4:1-35, 5:13, 5:14-19, 6:7, 6:14-23, 6:8-13, 6:24-30, 7:1-6, 7:11-34, 8:14-17, 8:18-21, 16:3-22, 16:24.

Now that you have accepted Christ as your Lord and Savior, you must allow him to live his life through you. This means that you must die in order for him to live. The sacrifice that has to be offered is now you! As you study the sacrifices of old you will see that God would not just accept anything. The sacrifice had to be without defect, blemish and most of all it had to cost the person something in order for God to accept it (See: Genesis chapter 4). Paul pleads with us in Romans 12:1, 2 NLT to present our bodies (our lives) to God, and let them be living and holy for this is the kind of sacrifice he will accept. Notice that this passage said that a holy sacrifice is the kind of sacrifice that God would accept. The word holy means **Holy** 1. [Sinless] devout, pious, blessed, righteous, moral, just, good, angelic, godly, reverent, venerable, immaculate, pure, spotless, clean, humble, saintly, innocent, god-like, saint-like, perfect, faithful, undefiled, untainted, chaste, upright, sanctified, spiritual. Believe it or not the list goes on. Quite a list huh? But there's a problem. The very first word in that definition was sinless! How can that be when humanity maintains that there is no way that we can live in these earthly bodies and live a sinfree life. God's word is very clear in that he commands us to be holy for he is holy (Leviticus 11:44&45) and to also be perfect just as he is. (Refer also to Matthew 5:48, I Thessalonians 4:7, I Peter 1:15&16). As a holy, spotless sacrifice for us, Jesus gave his very life that we may live. He died for us so that we wouldn't have to. The word die means to perish, come to nothing, or to come to nothing over a period of time. In a later chapter I give an illustration on how to kill something that is living. The answer is simple, don't feed it! Paul declares to us in I Corinthians that we also must die daily. This means that everyday (daily) we deny our flesh its sinful desires until we come forth looking exactly like our father, HOLY. To deny our flesh its sinful desires is not always an easy thing but God promises that if we loose our life in this world then we will find it, but if we seek to save our life we will loose it (Matthew 10:39, Luke 17:33, John 12:25). The New Living Translation reads like this in John 12:25 *"Those who love their life in this world will loose it. Those who despise their life in this world will keep it for eternal life"*. There is no way around it we will all die! Either in this life or the world to come, but we will die. Scripture is very clear in that it is appointed unto man (humanity) once to die and then the judgment (Hebrews 9:27).

For years many have been misinformed about what dying really means. When a loved one leaves this earthly realm we say they died when in fact God considers them asleep (See: Matthew 9:24,

Luke 8:52, John 11:11, Acts 7:60, I Corinthians 15:18). To die (to yourself) means to cease to do things according to your will and to allow God to live his life through you according to His will. I don't have any magical answer for you in response to the question "how do I die?" In fact, the answer is quite simple. You die by literally and consciously refusing your flesh what it wants that is contrary to the law and word of God. Paul said it best when he said, *"I discipline my body like an athlete, training it to do what it should"* (I Corinthians 9:27a NLT). Those that desire fruit in their life that will remain; dying is not an option. Unless that which you sow dies there can be no resurrection (I Corinthians 15:36). For some reason we tend to think that God's plan for our life is tedious, but it's quite the contrary. Every instruction we receive from God is to give us a quality life, a life that lasts far beyond this present world. To die to yourself does not mean that you have to give up all of your hopes and dreams. What it does mean is that instead of trying to figure out a plan for your life, you yield to the plan God already has for you. Instead of trying to use your own strength to make things happen for you, you rest in God's strength that will work toward you.

Because God's ways are far above our ways and likewise his thoughts there are times when we may feel that our dreams and desires are the least of God's concerns. This is when your trust in God must stand tall. Trust is not being fearful of the outcome or the future. The more you commune with God and are in his presence the more your trust in him will develop. When the relationship between God and yourself matures, you will find that your fears will begin to diminish. You will come to know him as a God that cannot lie (Numbers 23:19, Titus 1:2, Hebrews 6:18) a God that will give you the desires of your heart (Psalm 37:4) and a God that will reward those that diligently seek him (Hebrews 11:6). For anyone that has ever fasted, gone on a diet or simply made up in their minds that they were going to do or not do something, they will tell you that when they first started it may have been hard but over a period of time, as they continued, it got easier. When you first make up your mind to die to yourself it may seem hard but the more you yield to God, the easier it will become. The word of God declares, and I truly believe, that if you die now you will never have to die again.

CHAPTER THREE

"What do you need to look back for?"

THE REBIRTH

To often the assumption is made that when someone accepts Christ into their life that they've been born again. For years these two subjects have been clumped together into one category but after careful study of the word of God I must say that I disagree that they are one in the same. Yes, these two events can occur simultaneously however, they occur a lot less often than some would like to believe. When you receive Christ into your life you have confessed with your mouth and you believe in your heart. When you're born again you cease from sin (according to God's word). Two separate events! One day I was discussing the word of God with a dear friend of mine and as she spoke, the lord began to open the eyes of my understanding concerning this subject. Because of the sin, or disobedience if you will, of the first Adam we (humanity) all enter this earthly realm in death (separated from God). *"Wherefore, by one man sin entered into the world, and death by sin; and so **death passed upon all men**, for that all have sinned:".* Although we enter this earthly realm by way of our mother, we are viewed in the eyes of God as dead...dead in sin (Ephesians 2:1-13, Colossians 1:21, 2:11-13). Therefore, when we receive Christ into our lives, we become new creatures (II Corinthians 5:17) God removes or blots out the handwriting of ordinances that were against us, which was contrary to us, and took it out of the way, nailing it (our sins) to the cross (Colossians 2:14). You have now passed from death (being separated from God) unto life (back in fellowship with God) Refer to John 5:24 and I John 3:14. You have now entered your first birth, which is the washing of water by the word (Ephesians 5:26). You received the word you heard and became regenerated, raised from the dead, by that same word. Now you have the ability to see or comprehend the things of God giving you the power to not only be a child of God but to become a Son of God (John 1:12). Nicodemus was a ruler of the Jews and one who had accepted and received the words of Jesus, yet it was him whom Jesus spake with concerning being born *again*. According to I John 3:9 once you are born of God or the Spirit of God you do not commit sin. True, holiness is a process but there should and must come a point and time when we become holy, a point and time when we cease from sin. I Peter 4:1 NLT talks about the physical sufferings that Jesus experienced and declares to us that when we make a decision to suffer for Christ what in fact we have decided to do is stop sinning. For a moment let's look at several groups of people. There are those that have confessed with their mouth that Jesus is lord and have a great and sincere desire to be in the family of God, yet they continue to sin after the flesh. Then we have those who don't seem to be concerned at all about having a relationship with God, declaring that in fact that there really isn't a God. There are those that once walked with God and then turned away from him. And then there is the one who is born again. Allow me, I ask, to take a minute to dissect each one of these groups of people.

As stated before in earlier chapters, there are some that will argue that the blood of Jesus covers their sinful lifestyle because a confession was made at some point in their life. Well, this brings us to the first group of people listed, who confessed with their mouth but never crucified their flesh but continued to work the works of iniquity (sin). Jesus addressed this group in Matthew 7:21-23 by declaring to them that he never knew them. He never became intimate with them because sin separates you from God (Isaiah 59:2). Some would say that this group of people never had anything to do with God in the first place that's why they got turned away but please with a open mind read Matthew 7:21-23.

These people had cast out devils, prophesied in Jesus' name and done many wondrous works. This group of people, contrary to popular belief, had to be a part of God at some point and time because the word of God declares that a kingdom divided against itself cannot stand (Matthew 12:25). This statement was made in response to the slanderous thoughts the Pharisees had against Jesus when he himself cast out a devil. Jesus went on to say that even if Satan's kingdom is divided against itself it could not stand. In other words, he (Jesus) could not cast out a devil if in fact he was a devil himself and neither could the group of people in question. When Jesus healed the man born blind, the question was posed by the Jewish leaders, "What did he to thee?" (John 9:26). After all debate was over, the conclusion was that they had to admit that if Jesus had not been of God he would not have been able to do this miracle (John 9:33). So scripture shows us that this group of people had at some point confessed Jesus as lord, giving them the power or authority to do these mighty acts. The problem with this group of people is that they became again entangled with the bondage of sin (II Peter 2:20). As a dog returns to his vomit, so they did (II Peter 2:22) and their latter end was worse than their beginning. Because of their sinful lifestyle they experienced death (separation from God). As stated so many times thus far, confession alone is not enough but a lifestyle of holiness is an absolute must. Without it no man will see God.

The next group of people I want to address are the ones who say they don't believe that there is a God. The word of God declares that God has taken his laws off of tablets of stone and placed them on tablets of our (humanity's) heart (Hebrew 8:10,11) not having a need to tell our neighbor to know the lord for he has made himself known to all. Romans 1:19, 20 NLT records, that the truth about God is known to them instinctively. From the time the world was created people have seen God's invisible qualities, his eternal power and divine nature so no one has any excuse for not knowing God. God has made himself known to all its humanity that will not retain him, rejecting such knowledge (Romans 1:28). There will be no excuse that will be able to stand when faced with the judgment of God. The world, in times past, went through a period of time when they did not believe that Jesus, the Son of God, was in fact who we professed to be resulting in their unbelief in him. However, John 1:29 reads, *"Behold the Lamb of God which taketh away the sin of the world".* Well, my question was what was the sin of the world? John 16:9 NLT states, *"The world's sin is unbelief in me"*. The work of the Holy Spirit is to lead humanity into all truth (John 16:13). So in turn God took away unbelief. He took away every excuse that humanity would dare to use when faced with an account of their life.

The next group of people we will discuss are those who walked with God for a time and then turned away from him. Some may be asking what is the difference between the first group discussed and this group. Well, the first group discussed really believes that they are still walking with God and believe that they are not in danger of eternal judgment. They whole-heartedly believe that if they continue positive confessions that "I'm saved because I've confessed and believe" that their eternal salvation is secure. However, the word of God says that Jesus became the author of eternal salvation unto them that obey (Hebrew 5:9). Now the current group of people we are discussing are no longer making a confession of Christ. This group openly admits that they are no longer walking with God. The only difference between these two groups of people is that one group continues to confess while the other doesn't but nevertheless, both groups returned to their lifestyle of sin. Now, the group that turned away from walking with God, or whom we call backsliders, really proves the whole basis for this book. If confession alone guarantees salvation, there would be no such thing as a backslider. He that endureth unto the end, the same shall be saved. The word backslider means one that has moved from their position with God indicating they were once with him. David was a mighty man of God and referred to as a man after God's own heart. In addition, he was chosen to be the father of the coming messiah (Luke 1:32, Jeremiah 23:5, Isaiah 16:5, 9:6,7, Psalm 132:11, II Samuel 7:11). Although David often times operated out of his flesh, he always had a heart to repent. That is what God is looking for, a heart that is willing to repent. If after you receive Christ into your life there is no real consequence because of our lifestyle, then why would David in Psalm 51 plead for God to create in him a clean heart and renew a right spirit within him? He went so far as to ask God not to cast him away from his presence and not to take his Holy Spirit from him. David knew that sin would separate him from God. The point is that repentance is an absolute must if you want to continue your intimacy with God. Sin will only drive you from his presence. For a moment look if you will at Jeremiah chapter 3. This entire chapter concerns the backsliding condition of Israel and Judah. In this chapter God begins by paralleling a natural marriage to that of the spiritual marriage of Christ and his bride, the church. The first question posed in Jeremiah 3:1 is "If a man put away his wife, and she go from him, and become another man's, shall he return unto her again?" Here, God is addressing the issue of adultery. Although his chosen people, Israel, had turned their back on God pursuing idols he yet pleaded to them for their return to him. As God pleads for their return, he reminds them that he is married unto them (verse 14). Just as in the natural there are certain requirements for a successful re-union, so it is in the spirit. God was very clear in letting them (Israel) know what the conditions were upon their return. Verse 13 of Jeremiah chapter 3 records, "Only acknowledge thine iniquity, that thou hast transgressed against the lord thy God, and hast scattered thy ways to the strangers under every green tree, and ye have not obeyed my voice, saith the lord". This is the condition, acknowledge or confess your faults, and turn (verse 14). God is yet pleading with every backslider to return unto him. If thou wilt confess your sins before God, he is faithful and just to forgive your sins and cleanse you from all unrighteousness (I John 1:9).

So far we've discussed those who confessed Jesus as lord but never turned from their lifestyle of sin, those who maintain that they don't believe in God and those who walked with God for a season and now openly admit that they have departed. This brings us to the born again believer. When you receive Christ into your life you receive a seed. That seed has to have time to develop, grow, and then come forth. During this time God's grace covers our downfalls, mistakes and sins. Until God's word becomes mature in our lives we WILL struggle with sin, however there is a time when we leave the sins of the flesh. According to I John 3:6-9 whosoever abideth in him (meaning God) sinneth not; whosoever sinneth hath not seen him (meaning God) neither known him. Little children, let no man deceive you, he that doeth righteousness is righteous, even as he (God) is righteous. He that committeth sin is of the devil; for the devil sinneth from the beginning. For this purpose the Son of God was manifested, that he might destroy the works of the devil. **Whosoever is born of God doth not commit sin;** for his seed (God's word, Luke 8:11) remaineth in him **and he cannot sin** because he is born of God. Notice here in I John

3:6-9 the <u>born again</u> believer is addressed when in John 1:12 the one being addressed is the one who <u>receives</u>. These scriptures are rarely dealt with and for some very hard to swallow however verse 10 NLT of the same book and chapter says that this is how we can tell who are the children of God and who are the children of the devil. Anyone who does not obey God's commands and does not love other Christians does not belong to God. I John 5:16-18 only echoes the word that was just quoted but this chapter included a very interesting point. We just read that those born of God sin not, right? Well, verse 16 of I John 5 says all unrighteousness is sin but notice that it continues on to say that there is a sin <u>NOT</u> unto death. Is a born again believer flawless? No. However they do not commit sins that lead to death. Many are already asking, what sins lead to death and which ones don't? As scripture has said, all unrighteousness is sin. Not obeying your pastor is a sin because God instructs us to do so in Hebrews 13:17. Paul, by inspiration of God, instructs us not to take another believer to court in I Corinthians 6:1-7. In fact he instructs believers to rather suffer loss (I Corinthians 6:7). To married couples, God commands that ye defraud not one the other except it is with consent in I Corinthians 7:5 because it leaves room for temptation from the enemy. Very few people visit the widows or orphans in their time of need but we are instructed to do so in James 1:27. Proverbs 22:26 states "Be not thou one of them that strike hands, or of them that are sureties for debts". What does that mean? In plain English, don't make contracts or obtain loans where you use collateral, or co-sign with anyone who does (Study Proverbs 22:26 NLT). Why? Proverbs 22:7 tells you why, because the rich rule over the poor and the borrower is servant to the lender and we are to be servant to no one but God. To some people these examples may have been a stretch but they are real areas that we as believers struggle with from day to day. Do you think, for one minute, that any of the above listed examples are worthy of death? Of course not but in God's eyes they are still considered sin, falling short. For generation after generation the phrase has been passed down that "sin is sin". Through the years as I heard this common phrase I knew and understood the meaning behind it which was (is) you're no better than me because we all sin but scripture doesn't agree with that common myth. Scripture tells us in I John 5:16, "If a man sin a sin that does not lead to death we should pray and God will give that person life. But there is a sin that leads

43

to death and I'm not saying you should pray for those who commit it". According to God's word all sin does not lead to death. Now we are faced with some very serious questions. One being that if the phrase "sin is sin" is in fact a true one, why will God give life to one that sins and death to another who sins? Because as we've clearly read all sin is not considered the same. Paul said to pray for such people that sin in a way that doesn't lead to death. All of the examples given are areas that yes we need to improve in but we are not in danger of eternal judgement because of them. Galatians 5:19-21 along with Romans 1:29-31 lists such sins that are worthy of death, some which are, fornication, adultery, lasciviousness, hatred, ungrateful, the loss of natural affection, idolatry, the unbelieving and the lists go on. (Romans 1:32) Refer also to Ephesians 5:3-5, Colossians 3:5, I Corinthians 6:9, I Timothy 1:9,10 and Revelations 21:8. By the power of God, you will not see a born again believer fornicating, committing adultery, stealing, lying, worshiping idols, getting drunk, committing murder, hating his neighbor, envying his neighbor etc. At this point in my life I firmly believe that God's word is the final authority. And the word of God says if you are born of

God you don't sin (I John 3:9, 5:18) and can't sin (I John 3:9b). There is no way we can quote the word of God that says "As he is so are we in this world" and still maintain that a sin free life is unobtainable. For years humanity has loved to feel that there is no way a sin free life could be lived but for that very reason did the Son of God come into this world, to defeat the one that held the power of <u>sin</u> and <u>death</u>. It's funny how boldly we will declare that just as Jesus healed the sick likewise we can. Just as Jesus commanded money to come from the mouth of a fish likewise we can. Just as Jesus fed five thousand with little to nothing likewise we can but the minute someone declares that just as Jesus lived in the flesh and sinned not likewise we can there is great disbelief and argument that pure holiness is obtainable. If after the work of the cross we have no more power than we did before the work of the cross then Jesus shed his blood in vain! Jesus has given us power through his blood to be as he is...HOLY.

We all have great room for improvement in our lives but just as Jesus lived in this flesh and lived a sin free life, so are we to walk. God is looking for holiness and we must get passed the sins of the flesh that lead to death in order to go on to perfection. Christ was an example for us that we should follow his steps (I Peter 2:21, 22). According to the word of God you can, through the power of God, live a sin free life.

HOW FINE IS THE LINE?

All things are lawful unto me, but all things are not expedient: all things are lawful for me, but I will not be brought under the power of any

I Corinthians 6:12

Many people feel that when the appeal goes forth for salvation that there are automatic restrictions. There are many excuses that we hear. Some say I'm not ready to give up this, some say I can't stop that. We prolong our call to salvation for so many different reasons. True the word of God does say count up the cost of discipleship before you "enter the race". But the problem is this, if God is the one who has chosen you and not you yourself, how do you know if you will ever get another chance to respond to a call from God? What people don't realize is that in Christ there is no bondage at all. Bondage comes when you are outside of the liberty of God. To live in sin is bondage but to live inside the arms of the almighty one is peace, joy, hope, security, life and liberty. For this very reason did the Son of God come into this world, to set at liberty them that are bruised and to deliver those that are held captive. Refer to Leviticus 25:10, Isaiah 61:1, Luke 4:18, Romans 8:21, Galatians 5:1 and James 1:25. God has called us to a life of liberty but not liberty to satisfy our sinful nature but liberty to serve one another in love (Galatians 5:13). God desires that his people live a life of quality. He has manifested himself that we may have life and that more abundantly. God has given us all things to enjoy but the problem comes when we go outside the guidelines he has set to try and find what we call "happiness". Many believe that an occasional drink is ok as long as they don't drink in access. Some believe that listening to secular music is ok. Many feel that going to a "party" every now and then is not harmful. The question is not are these beliefs wrong or right, the question is, are these beliefs beneficial to our Christian walk. Is this liberty that you are walking in becoming a stumbling block to someone else? The word of God says in I Corinthians 8:9 *"But take heed lest by any means this liberty of yours become a stumbling block to them that are weak"*. (Refer also to Romans 14:13). Anyone who has ever run in any type of race or dared to grace a walking trail will tell you that you shouldn't wear a lot of heavy clothing or eat a heavy meal directly prior to the event. You can't even carry a lot of things with you while participating in these activities. Runners and health conscious people will also tell you that prior to the respectful event they begin to prepare themselves, their physical bodies, by watching what they eat. Cutting back on certain foods while maybe increasing in others. They are free to eat and drink whatever they want but they know that although they have this liberty all things are not beneficial to the goal they are reaching for. Depending upon what this person wants to accomplish will determine how well or consistent they will be in following the guidelines that have been set. *"Endure suffering along with me, as a good soldier of Christ Jesus. And as Christ's soldier, do not let yourself become tied up in the affairs of this life, for then you cannot satisfy the one who has enlisted you in his army. Follow the lord's rules for doing his work, just as an athlete either follows the rules or is disqualified and wins no prize"* (II Timothy 2:3-5 NLT) First natural, then spiritual. We have been given liberty in all things but not all things are beneficial to our Christian walk. The lord commands that we come out from among them and be ye separate (II Corinthians 6:17).

There must be a distinction between the church (the body of Christ) and the world. For some the "line" is to fine, but if we would look through the eyes of God we will see that life can be enjoyed to the fullest without bondage, without compromise and without perversion. When God created humanity, he gave them power over all things (Genesis 1:26) but the problem came when man went outside the guidelines that had been set. Man (humanity) when he sinned experienced death (separation from God) removing him from his state of dominion but as we return to God he restores us to our original state, which is headship in the earth, to enjoy all things. The narrow road, though it seems restricted, leads to life and liberty in Christ Jesus, while the broad road leads to death and destruction. Everything we want, God wants for us as well but he demands we find it all in him.

BY THIS SIGN

By this shall all men know that ye are my disciples, if ye have love one to another.
                    John 13:35

When God established the new covenant, he fulfilled all the law inside one (the greatest) commandment, which is love (Matthew 22:35-

40). Throughout the years the word love has been thoroughly redefined. Romans 13:8 states, *"He that loveth another hath fulfilled the law"*. What I focused on was Romans 13:10 that states, love worketh no ill towards his neighbor: Therefore love is the fulfilling of the law. Notice that the word of God did not say that by this shall all men know that you are my disciples by how many hugs and kisses you greet men with. It didn't say that men would know that we are his disciples by how polite we are or even if we give to the poor. So what was Jesus really saying in John 13:35? If you love your neighbor you will not sleep with their spouse (adultery). If you love your neighbor you will not cause deathly harm to them (murder). If you love your neighbor you will not wrongly take their belongings (steal). If you love your neighbor you will not falsely accuse them (lie). Get the picture? So in turn what Jesus was really saying was all men would know that you are my disciples by the way you conduct yourselves. Love is not something you do; it's something you become. As children of God we are to become who he is and God is love. There really isn't any subject that can be addressed without discussing holiness. Holiness is the attribute that will tell or show all men that you are God's own. Not a hug, not a kiss, not a polite word, not a treat to dinner but pure holiness. Of course these actions are byproducts of the love you have one to another. Humanity calls it affection, which is much different from true love. This kind of conduct was addressed in I Corinthians 13:1-13. Notice that this group of people spoke with tongues, prophesied, understood great mysteries and knowledge, had great faith and gave to the poor yet scripture said that all of that could be done without love.

CHAPTER FOUR

"You can do whatever you believe you can do"

I CAN'T GIVE IT UP!

And he said to them all, If any man will come after me, let him deny himself, and take up his cross daily, and follow me.

St. Luke 9:23

Deny: *disagree with, disallow, not admit, and say no to*

WEBSTER'S NEW WORLD THESAURUS

Deny: *to refuse to grant*

WEBSTER'S ELEMENTARY DICTIONARY

In times past humanity was bound or held captive by sin through the law. It was through the law that sin received its power (I Corinthians 15:56 NLT). However God, through the death of his son Jesus, has given us victory or power over sin and death   (I Corinthians 15:57 NLT). Unlike our ancestors who constantly struggled with sin having no power or strength to overcome, we've been given power through the shed blood of Jesus Christ. *"So this is the point: The law no longer holds you in its power, because you died to its power when you died with Christ on the cross"* (Romans 7:4 NLT). The word of God now contends that we (humanity) are drawn away (from him) when we are tempted with or by our own lust. In other words now that the blood of Jesus gives us power over sin to be no more servant to it, the excuse of "I couldn't help myself" is no longer valid. Luke in chapter 9 and verse 23 of his volume declares that if any man wants to be a follower of Jesus he must first deny himself, take up his cross and follow him.

One definition for deny, is to refuse to grant. The flesh will always desire the things that are opposite of what God wants for our lives but we must refuse to grant our flesh what it wants. Until we come to a point where we die to ourselves, the flesh will always war against the spirit. How do you kill any living thing? One way is to cease to feed it. If you don't feed your kids, they will die. If you don't feed your pets, they will die. If you don't feed your plants, they will die. If you continually don't feed your flesh, it WILL die. The word die means to perish or come to nothing. Perish means to return to the original state of being. If someone asks you to bring a non-perishable item of course you wouldn't take a box of chocolate or any type of candy. Why? Because it will eventually return to sugar form because sugar is what it originated from. Paul admonishes us to die daily. What does that mean? What was the original state of the flesh?

It was in total submission to the Spirit. Through the atoning work of the cross, Jesus has set us free from the law of sin and of death not to serve sin any more but to become servants of righteousness. In fact the word tells us that just as we were once slaves or servants to sin we must now become slaves or servants to righteousness and holiness (Romans 6:19). The same energy we used when we were in our sinful state to serve sin should be the same energy we use in our lively state to serve righteousness. When we were in our sinful state we only had death to look forward to but now being made free from sin we have fruit unto holiness to look forward to which will lead us to eternal life (Romans 6:21,22).

So now that we've been given power over sin the question is posed, why are there so many people professing to be followers of Christ who still continue in sin? For so long the story has been told that the work of Calvary covers our life of sin when in fact the work of Calvary gave us power to live holy before God. To love the lord is to hate evil (Psalm 97:10) and the fear of the lord is also to hate evil (Proverbs 8:13). The bottom line is that the fear or reverence for God is gone from our society today. Grace is not a license to continue in sin but grace and mercy come to purge (clean out and remove) us from iniquity and when men fear the lord you know it because they depart from evil (Proverbs 16:6). There is a way that seemeth right to man but the end thereof is death.

The highway of the upright is to depart from evil (Proverbs 16:17). The enemy would love to keep you bound believing that there is no way you could ever let go of the issues in your life but God, who is greater than all, has given us power over all things. I guarantee that if you launch out whole-heartedly in God you will soon come to realize that you can live the life God is calling you to. This day settle in your heart that you can and will let every thing go that is not pleasing to God. What would it profit a man to gain the whole world and loose his soul? Remember that the pleasure of sin is only for a season but the pay for it is eternal. The persecution of the righteous is only for a season but the reward of it is eternal as well. Whatever the issue, it's not worth eternity!

THE AUTHOR'S TESTIMONY

As one who was raised by two pastors, it seems as if I always had a great love and desire for God. In the household that I grew up in there was always some scripture being quoted, a song being sung or a Christian radio or TV show playing. Because of this type of influence, I received Christ into my life at a very young age, the age of 8. Throughout my life I saw many signs and wonders. The laying on of hands, devils (literal) being cast out and many prayers of faith were being released over the lives of people. Having two parents who were pastors we always found ourselves in a church service. Therefore I "heard" the word of God constantly but there came a time in my life when I had to move from relying on the relationship my parents had with God and begin to develop a relationship with God myself. As often as I felt the tug of God, I tried to yield. I began reading and meditating more and more on the word of God until I could see growth (spiritual growth) in myself. As I began to grow in God I not only could quote the word but I began to understand it and soon came revelation of it.

By the time I was 18 I had birthed a child out of wedlock, traveled the world and re-settled in Oklahoma. Upon my returning to Oklahoma I reunited with a childhood sweetheart, which produced my second child out of wedlock. That relationship resulted in a very rocky marriage in which I became exposed to verbal, emotional and sometimes physical abuse. Like many people, I tried to drown my sorrows by turning to marijuana and liquor. Eventually that marriage ended. I had gotten so far away from the things my parents had taught me. I needed God like I never had before. There were nights I cried wanting change in my life. Wanting the life my parents had always told me to strive to have. Although my childhood was not a flawless one I was always taught to put God first in everything I do and that's what I had gotten away from. The more I cried out to God I could hear the words "Draw nigh to me and I will draw nigh to thee". I remember feeling the presence of God in my life again and I purposed in my heart to get back on track. One day during a Sunday morning service my pastor, at that time, opened the altar and extended an invitation to all those that felt the call of God on their life for ministry. I gripped the pew in front of me while having a conversation with God. Thinking within myself, there's no way God can use me after all I've done. I heard the voice of the lord say, yes I can and I will. With that I found myself out of my seat and at the altar. As the service progressed I felt commissioned by God to go forth and do what it was he was calling me to do…preach the gospel. I left that day with a great sense of purpose and determination. I increased in reading my bible, praying and seeking God. I sought God until at last I began to hear his voice clear. The summer of 1998 I heard the lord say go! I prayed for an answer as to where I was to go and why it was even necessary for me to leave where I was. It was months later that I found out why but the where was South Carolina. It was there that my ministry actually started. The lord had placed me under a beautiful ministry that would allow me to exercise my gift. I was sent there for a reason and a purpose and the lord would not release me to come home until that purpose had been fulfilled. Later, I would find out that I was sent there to receive power to go through. January 27, 1999 I received the baptism of the Holy Spirit. At that point in my life I really was walking with God. I had gotten built up in the word and was running the Christian race with patience, I thought. I had overcome many obstacles in my life and was overwhelmed at where God had me at that point in my life. Little did I know that upon my returning back to Oklahoma I would experience one of the most devastating times of my life. I continued moving forward in the ministry. I was teaching Sunday school as well as Wednesday night bible studies. I was preaching Sunday morning messages and was head of auxiliaries in the church. I was doing street ministry and was an active member of a minister's alliance that had formed. I was very active in the work of the lord. Sounds good huh? In the midst of all of that, six months after my return home I found myself in an adulterous affair. What could have gone wrong? My life was literally upside down. I could not believe that once again God's word in my life had become just that, words. My life was no longer adorning the nature and character of God. The day I fell I remember feeling so empty. Immediately I said to myself never again but what I wasn't aware of is that an instant soul tie and strong hold had taken place that would hold me captive for two years. Trying to "keep face" I continued my duties at the church going so far as to receive my license as a minister of the gospel. Because of my background in the church and the level of word I already had it was possible for me to stand before a crowd and expound on various scriptures while all the time my life was a living hell. This behavior could only last for a season before I began drawing back from the ministry. As the sin in my life grew stronger and stronger I could no longer stand before God's people. The shame and guilt would overtake me. I grew farther and farther away from the God I knew could deliver me. I had been overtaken by the grip of death. I was afraid to leave my house by car fearing I would have a wreck and die. I was afraid to let someone else drive fearing they would wreck. I was afraid to go to sleep fearing that I would not see morning. My whole life was now consumed in fear. I had removed myself from the perfect love, which is God, which would cast out all of my fears. As I began to try and find my way back to God, the enemy put forth his best foot.

All that I could imagine wanting I began receiving through this sinful relationship. It didn't matter if it was money, clothes, bills paid, furniture or a weekend get away I got what I wanted. But the things did not fill the void that had taken over my life. I was now faced with a decision... do I enjoy the pleasures of sin and loose my eternal soul or do I seek a glorious reward? I lingered in this state for far to long until one day through a precious prophetess of God I received the words "Set your house in order, for you will die". When I received that word I immediately fell to the floor. She had only confirmed what the lord was already telling me. I knew all my life that the wages of sin was death but now it's at my door, looking me straight in the eyes. As I fell to the floor I could not remember ever being that broken before God. I cried out to God to spare my life. Many people say that when they are about to die whether it's from a car wreck, a robbery or an illness their life flashes before them. I can truly say that as I cried to the lord, my life literally flashed before me as well. At that time I had 4 children the youngest being only four and a half. I called her to my side as tears streamed down my face. I sat her in my lap and began to ask her about all the things and places she remembered us going and doing. As she kicked her feet off the end of my lap she softly said, "I don't know". I said, "Do you remember when we went to South Carolina?" she said, "No". I asked, "Do you remember when we spent the summer with papa in Tulsa" she said, "No". I put her on the floor and told her to go back in the front with the rest of the kids. I said to God, lord if you take my life now my baby wouldn't even remember me. At that time my oldest child was only 12 years old. So many times the comment is made "it's my life; I can do what I want. Who's it hurting?" But as I looked over my life I was saddened by how many lives had been affected because of a decision I made and how many lives would be destroyed if I didn't do something about the sinful state I was in. My heart was broke. I sent message to the prophetess that had spoken the word of death and asked her to pray for me. She did as I requested and the word came back to me, "If you will truly repent God will spare your life". It was at that very moment that I made up in my mind that no matter what I had to do to keep my life I would do it. So often I had heard the story of the prodigal son returning home but at this point in my life I was so far away from God I didn't know how to get back to him. All I knew was that the relationship that I was in had to end. It was a consistent battle for several months after I explained to the man I was involved with that the relationship could not continue, but I stood by my commitment to God. It was weeks that I did nothing but seek to hear God's voice again. Forgiveness from God was instant but the restoration period took some time. I remember like yesterday when God restored me to his family. As a newborn baby is cleaned from all the nastiness that they have lived in for months, so felt I. It was like God wiped me from head to toe. That day, September 16, 2001, I know that I had not just been reunited with God but something more had taken place. I had finally been *born again.*

Up until now I had only received Jesus into my life. I had confessed him with my mouth and

I truly did believe that God had raised him from the dead. I loved him but not enough to crucify and deny my sinful flesh its evil desires. From the time I received Christ into my life to the time I actually got born again I continually struggled with sin. I would fall and get up. Fall and get up. But there came a time when I became what God said I could be, holy. Do I believe that every thing I went through served a purpose in my life? Most definitely! But now that I've been enlightened, experienced the good things of heaven and shared in the Holy Spirit, tasted of the goodness of the word of God and the power of the age to come, I'm determined more than ever to never return to the former life I once lived. Since the day of my birth, the sins of the flesh are not even an option for me any more. When God delivered me he told me that he delivered me from the spirit and not the man so in whatever form that spirit may come in I'm delivered from it. I quickly moved my membership from the church I had attended and sought God as to where he would have me go. He directed me to place where I truly did find hope and victory. Although I was back on track and once again had a zeal for God I still could not fully understand why God allowed me to experience such a traumatic time in my life.

One day during a morning service my pastor stood graced behind the pulpit and spoke such profound words, which were "God will allow you to go through a thing to bring you to a greater revelation of it". It was then that God answered my question of why? Scripture after scripture began to flood my mind as God began to unfold what he wanted me to see the whole time. It was simply this that if I had died in my sinful state all of the preaching, teaching, evangelism, etc. I had done would not have been enough to secure my eternal fate. Hell would have been my permanent and eternal dwelling place. My confession at the age of 8 would not have secured my eternal salvation. I had to be born again. I had to come to a place where I crucified my flesh and ceased from sin because without holiness no man shall see God and he has no respect of persons so I knew that included me. Because of God's love and mercy for me my love for him has grown to heights unknown. Am I flawless now? No! But now that my flesh is crucified I can move on to perfection. If throughout my life I've learned nothing more I have learned that "Not everyone that saith unto me lord, lord shall enter into the kingdom but he that doeth the will of the father". Please I beg you, be not deceived! Whatever you sow that will you also reap. If you sow to the flesh you <u>will</u> reap to the flesh corruption, but if you sow to the spirit you <u>will</u> of the spirit reap eternal life. Eternal life is our ultimate goal. Don't be as one who gained the whole world and lost his soul. *I don't mean to say that I have already achieved these things or that I have already reached perfection! But I keep working towards that day when I will finally be all that Christ Jesus saved me for and wants me to be. No, dear brothers and sisters, I am still not all I should be, but I am focussing all my energies on this one thing: Forgetting the past and looking forward to what lies ahead. I strain to reach the end of the race and receive the prize for which God, through Christ Jesus, is calling us up to heaven.* (Philippians 3:12-14 NLT). My prayers are with you all.

WHAT IS MY FATE AS A BACKSLIDER?

Let the one who is doing wrong continue to do wrong; the one who is vile, continue to be vile; the one who is good, continue to do good; and the one who is holy, continue in holiness.
Revelation 22:11 NLT

This chapter is one that is very dear to my heart because there came a time in my life when I had to ask myself the very same question. If I had died in the state I was in, what would have been my fate as a backslider? I was reminded of the story of the ten virgins in Matthew 25. Five of these virgins were wise and five were unwise in the fact that they had not fully prepared for their journey ahead. When it was time for the virgins to be united with the bridegroom, only five were prepared. The other five desired to enter into the chamber as well but the door had been shut and they could not enter in. Notice that while all ten virgins was together no one was able to tell who the wise ones were and who the unwise ones were. It was only after a period of separation. Matthew 25 tells us that the Son of Man (Jesus) will sit on his throne and as a shepherd he will separate the sheep from the goats. The one's denied entrance into the kingdom of God is the goats. The one's that gained entrance is the sheep. By now you should be convinced that God requires we endure to the end or finish our course. Ten virgins started out on the journey but only five finished. We must be prepared to stay on the road that God has placed us on. *For when people escape from the wicked ways of the world by learning about our lord and savior Jesus Christ and then get tangled up with sin and become it's slave again, they are worse off than before. It would be better if they had never known the right way to live than to know it and then reject the Holy commandments that were given to them* (II Peter 2:20,21 NLT).

When Jesus was faced with the question "Lord, will only a few be saved?" Jesus responded, the door to heaven is narrow. Work hard to get in, because many will try to enter, but when the head of the house has locked the door, it will be too late. Then you will stand outside knocking and pleading, "lord, open the door for us!" but he will reply, "I do not know you" you will say, "but we ate and drank with you, and you taught us in our streets". And he will reply, "I tell you, I don't know you. Go away, all you who do evil." (Luke 13:23-27 NLT) So the answer was yes! Only a few will be saved according to Matthew 7:13&14. The word of God declares that when the Son of Man returns, it will be as it was in the days of Noah. In those days, before the flood, people were enjoying banquets and parties and weddings right up to the time Noah entered the ark. People didn't realize what was going to happen until the flood came and swept them all away. That is the way it will be when the Son of Man comes. Be prepared is the plea in verse 42 of Matthew 24 NLT because no man knows the day nor the hour when the Son of Man shall return. If you are outside the ark of safety when the head of the house returns, the door will be shut and you will find yourself eternally cast from the presence of God.

Jude pleads with us to defend the gospel given to us because there are some godless people who have come in among us declaring that God's forgiveness allows us to live immoral lives. We know that is indeed not a fact. Should we keep on sinning so that God can show us more and more kindness and forgiveness? Of course not! Since we have died to sin, how can we continue to live in it? Jude goes on to discuss the fate awaiting those who continue in sin after receiving God's truth.

One scripture that I found very eye opening for me is Ezekiel chapters 18 and 33 which really only echo each other. They declare that if you sin after you receive your righteous position it is possible for you to loose that righteousness and die for the sin you've committed. Let's just see what it says! Ezekiel 33:12-20 NIV reads, *"Therefore, son of man, say to your countrymen, The righteousness of the righteous man will not save him when he disobeys, and the wickedness of the wicked man will not cause him to fall when he turns from it. The righteous man, if he sins, will not be allowed to live because of his former righteousness. If I tell the righteous man that he will surely live, but then he trusts in his righteousness and does evil, none of the righteous things he has done will be remembered; he will die for the evil he has done. And if I say to the wicked man, you will surely die, but he then turns away from his sin and does what is just and right—if he gives back what he took in pledge for a loan, returns what he has stolen, follow the decrees that give life, and does no evil, he will surely live; he will not die. None of the sins he has committed will be remembered against him. He has done what is just and right; he will surely live. Yet your countrymen say,"The way of the lord is not just". But it is their way that is not just. If a righteous man turns from his righteousness and does evil, he will die for it. And if a wicked man turns away from his wickedness and does what is just and right, he will live by doing so. Yet, O house of Israel, you say, "The way of the lord is not just". But I will judge each of you according to his own ways.*

There is no way around it; our righteousness must be maintained until the end. The scripture is clear, this man was indeed righteous! How do you become righteous? By accepting and receiving Christ into your life. This man did just that and yet God said in the day that a righteous man sins, he will die for the sin he has committed and his former righteousness will be remembered no more. In my opinion, the reason this man fell away is not as important as the fact that he was indeed righteous and then returned to sin. He died for his sin and lost his righteousness or his righteous position. God tells us in Revelation 3:15, 16 that he wants us hot or cold, not lukewarm. Many feel that their eternal salvation is secured regardless of the lifestyle lived after confession. However, in the same chapter of Revelation verse 5 there is a reference to a blotting away of names from the book of life. *"He that overcometh, the same shall be clothed in white raiment; and I will not blot out his name out of the book of life, but I will confess his name before my father, and before his angels".* What was interesting to me was that the Webster's New World Thesaurus had two definitions for the word blot. It also had a definition for the word blot out, which is. Blot out v. [To mark out] deface, cross out, scratch out, delete; see also cancel. Some believe that this is not giving reference to a literal blotting out nor a literal book of life but whatever the case it is a fact that God will blot you out or cancel you from his memory and promise because of sin. It's funny to me that when God begins talking about "blotting out" our sins (Psalm 51:1, Isaiah

43:25, Acts 3:19) we take that literal. We boldly confess that we've been forgiven and that our sins are no longer remembered because of <u>this</u> blotting out but it's hard to grasp the concept of God blotting out our names from the book of life. The fact remains these people will not receive the promise of God, which is eternal life.

God is a God of longsuffering! Everyone has a processing time. My prayer is that you don't let time run out before you choose to repent. God is calling to every backslider to return to him. He reminds us in his word that he is married unto the backslider (Jeremiah 3:14). What does that mean? It means that God is going to keep the promise he made to you that if you hear his voice, open your heart and repent he will receive you again unto himself. When you feel the presence of God overshadowing your life, harden not your heart. *Because I have called, and ye refused; I have stretched out my hand, and no man regarded; but ye have set at naught all my council, and would none of my reproof: I also will laugh at your calamity: I will mock when your fear cometh* (Proverbs 1:25,26). In the state of a backslider, your fate is eternal separation from the presence of God. This separation will be considered and referred to as the second death (Revelation 20:6, 20:11-15, 21:8). We had no control over the first death we experienced, we received that death because of the first Adam (Romans 5:12-21) but we do have control over the second death. God declares by his written word that if we hear his words and believe on him that we have passed from death to life and will not come into condemnation (John 5:24, I John 3:14). If, in fact, we die in an un-repented state, as a backslider, our fate will be the eternal damnation of our soul (Ezekiel 18, 33, Daniel 12:2, John 5:28, 29, Mark 9:43-48). The key is to not give up! There is still hope, if you confess your sins, he is faithful and just to forgive you and cleanse you from all unrighteousness. That confession will place you back in fellowship with the father. Shake yourself, forget the past and press toward the destiny God has for you.

CHAPTER FIVE

"Receive the end of your faith"

WHERE MY ROAD LEADS

Enter ye in at the straight gate: for wide is the gate, and broad is the way, that leadeth to destruction, and many there be which go in thereat: Because straight is the gate, and narrow is the way, which leadeth unto life, and few there be that find it.

Matthew 7:13, 14

Have you ever desired to take a trip somewhere then remembered that someone you know had already been there? Have you ever asked someone for directions on how to get to a specific place? When you received the instructions did they tell you things to look for along the way? Jesus has traveled the road that we are now on and desire to finish. He walked the earth in flesh (II Timothy 3:16) and then entered into the most holy place, God's sanctuary (Hebrews 6:19, 20 NLT). God desires that we all follow in the path of his dear son, Jesus; however he leaves the choice to us (Deuteronomy 30:19). It is not God's will that any should perish but that all would come to repentance (II Peter 3:9). Salvation, through holiness, is not somewhere we just end up. We, as believers, are instructed to "strive" or "work" to enter into the straight gate. In other words, it's a conscious effort that must be made on our part. What we as a people fail to realize is that repentance is an absolute must in order to remain on this road of life (Luke 13:3). For some reason there seems to be a misconception about the life of a Christian. Many feel that a Christian lives a life of ease. A life of peace, yes! A life of ease, no! God's word is clear about two things concerning the life of a Christian. One, in order to be a follower of Christ we must first deny ourselves and take up our cross (Mark 8:34). This means that as a follower of Christ we will experience pain just as Jesus did. Two, God has given us access to his kingdom (his glory, power & authority) but through much tribulation shall we obtain it (Acts 14:22). We must renew our minds and come to a place where we drop the mentality of wanting something for nothing. We all want God's best, we all desire heaven but at no cost to us. Christ told us that if we suffer with him then we would also reign with him (II Timothy 2:12). At this point some may be thinking this doesn't sound like a life you want to live. The thought of hurting and suffering is not appeasing to you but may I suggest something? Whether you suffer with Christ or without him, you will suffer. This earthly life is full of pain and suffering. The difference between one who suffers with

Christ and the one who suffers without Christ is the love and protection a father gives to his own as well as his rewards. Those who suffer with Christ know that God is the good shepherd (John 10:11) and we have protection through him from anything that may come against us while doing the work of the father (Psalm 91). Those suffering without Christ do not have access to this same protection. God, through his son Jesus, invites all that labor and are heavy laden to come unto him and he will give them rest. He says in Matthew 11:28-30 *"Take my yoke upon you, and learn of me. For my yoke is easy and my burden light"*. Notice that Jesus did not deny that you were still going to have burdens but now that we are yoked together with Christ we have assistance with everything we face in this life. One of the biggest obstacles in the life of a Christian is to not get weary in the race. Contrary to popular opinion, Christians (believers) still hurt, get tired, cry, get disappointed and have emotions just like the next person. What keeps us pressing beyond all of that is the reward we know awaits us. He that cometh to him must believe that he is and that he is a rewarder of them that diligently seek him (Hebrews 11:6b). Does the reward consist of heaven alone? No! There is no man that hath left house, or brethren, or sisters, or father, or mother, or wife, or children, or lands, for my sake, and the gospel's, But he shall receive an hundred-fold now in this time, houses, and brethren, and sisters, and mother's, and children, and lands, with persecution: and in the world to come eternal life (Mark10: 29, 30) See also Matthew 19:29.

There is a way that seemeth right unto a man but the end thereof are the ways of death (Proverbs 14:12). If you were traveling down an interstate highway and noticed that you were going the wrong direction what would you do? Maybe you would stop and get directions or maybe you would just turn around. The word of God is a road map that will lead us into the very place where Jesus now is, the presence of the Almighty God. Along this road Jesus has given us specific things to look for that will ensure that we are on the right path. By this shall all men know that you are my disciples, or followers, by the love you have one for another. Love is the main sign that we need to look for. Since God is love we know that love is the path that leads to life. Love consists of many elements. If we love God, we will keep his commandments, if we love our neighbor we will work no ill to him and eventually the fruit of the Spirit will be evident in our lives which is: Joy, peace, long suffering, temperance etc. (Galatians 5:22-24). Some of you don't see any of the signs that are listed on the road map, which is the word of God. God is standing waiting for your call. Jeremiah 33:3 says "Call unto me, and I will show thee great and mighty things, which thou knowest not". It's not to late for you to stop, get more directions and turn around. Repent! Rethink your position and turn from. This is the message Jesus preached while he walked this earth. It was the basis of his whole ministry (Matthew 4:17, Mark 1:15, 6:12).

When we really die to ourselves and obey God the way he commands us to the blessings will overtake us. In my opinion, the joy, peace and rewards I receive from doing the work of my father far exceed the sufferings I may have to endure. Even Jesus, when faced with the death of the cross, looked ahead to a future joy. Hebrews 12:2 NLT encourages us by stating *"We do this by keeping our eyes on Jesus, on whom our faith depends from start to finish. He was willing to die a shameful death on the cross because of the joy he knew would be his afterward. Now he is seated in the place of highest honor beside God's throne in Heaven".* Do I get excited about the "things" in this life? Yes! Just as anyone else, I enjoy nice things. Is that where my joy lies? Absolutely not! My joy comes from knowing that it pleases God that I prosper in this life (Psalm 35:27, Luke 12:32) and I don't have to compromise my soul for it. The joy comes from knowing that I can enjoy life here in this realm and I will still one-day see my Savior face to face and forever be in his presence.

<u>THE REWARD</u>

And, behold, I come quickly; and my reward is with me, to give every man according as his work shall be.

Revelation 22:12

Contrary to popular belief, the reward a Christian seeks is not a car, a house, good job or riches. The reward we seek, and are promised, is eternal life (Romans 6:23). Instead of seeking an eternal reward, which is life itself, what much of humanity has done, and is doing, is seeking temporal rewards. We as a people have gotten caught up in the glamour of this life when the word clearly warns us against doing so in Matthew 6:19, 20. We are not to lay up treasures on earth where moth and rust do corrupt but rather lay up treasures in heaven. In other words, seek the things that will last...life (I Peter 1:3-

5). Do we ever stop and think about the price Jesus paid in order for us to have life? The price he paid was his own life. So often we belittle this act of love. What if we never get a new car? What if we never become homeowner's? What if we never attain the status in life we desire? These reasons are not why Jesus came and shed his precious blood. Christ died to redeem humanity from death, forgive us of our sins, give us peace, and bring us back together with the father and ultimately to rescue us from the penalty of death. (Ephesians 1:7, Colossians 1:20, II Corinthians 1:9, John 5:24, Acts 2:24, Romans 6:9, 8:2, Hebrews 2:9, I John 3:14).

Because we love God and keep his commandment (love) we look to that day when we will reign together with him in the glorious kingdom of heaven. God promises us that his son has gone to prepare a place for us that where he is there we may be also (John 14:2, 3). That promise holds fast still today! Jesus went away (Acts 1:11 NLT) and he will return one day to receive all those who look for his glorious appearing (Matthew 24:30,31NLT, Acts 3:20, 21 NLT, Titus 2:11-13, II Peter 3:13,14, Colossians 3:4, I Corinthians 1:7,8 15:23 I Thessalonians 1:10, 4:13-18, Revelation 1:5-8). While we remain in this earthly realm, we remain subject to sin and temptation, which can deter us from the things of God. The word of God cautions us not to be tossed to and fro with every wind of doctrine (Ephesians 4:14, Hebrews 13:9). God spoke these words through his servants because he knew that in this life some would leave the faith. Many will leave sound doctrine and begin to give heed to doctrines of devils (I Timothy 4:1, 2). Once Christ returns to receive us unto himself, there will be no more mention of a "backslider". We will no longer be trapped in the body of death. Just as humanity lived in harmony with God in the beginning so shall we also when Christ appears. We will *then* be rescued (SAVED) from the presence, pain and penalty of sin. We will be clothed with an immortal body (I Corinthians 15:39-54, Philippians 3:20, 21) suitable to behold the very glory of God. The reward of heaven far exceeds anything tangible we may receive in this life. Time is far spent for us to re-evaluate the reward we want to receive. Is God not more than a car? house? Riches? Fame? What you receive in this life is temporal, what God desires you to have is eternal. What would it profit a man if he gain the whole world and loose his soul? Seek God above the things. *"After all, what gives us hope and joy, and what is our proud reward and crown? It is you! Yes, you will bring us much joy as we stand together before our lord Jesus when he comes back again. For you are our pride and joy"* I Thessalonians 2:19, 20 NLT. According to I Peter 1:9 NLT, our reward for trusting God will be the salvation of our souls.

WHY LATER?

And when the chief Shepherd shall appear, ye <u>shall</u> receive a crown of glory that fadeth not away

I Peter 5:4 KJV

And when the head Shepherd comes, your reward <u>will be</u> a never-ending share in his glory and honor.

I Peter 5:4 NLT

As I've stated so many times in earlier chapters, our greatest desire as Christians should be to lay eyes on and behold face to face the one that gave his son that we might have life. As long as we remain in this earthly realm that will never happen. Scripture declares that no man has seen God at any time (John 1:18, 6:46, I Timothy 6:16, I John 4:12). I John 4:12 states that if we love one another then God is seen <u>through</u> us but I believe, according to scripture, that one day, when we pass from this life, we will see our

Savior, our Lord, our God face to face. No man can see God and live (Exodus 33:20) the mortal bodies we live in cannot contain the glory of God. When Moses inquired to God about seeing his glory God placed him in the cleft of a rock, covered his face, passed in front of him and just in time for him to behold his back parts God removed his hand from his face (Exodus 33:17-23). Although these mortal bodies cannot behold the glory of God, we can rest assure that one-day this mortal will put on immortality (I Corinthians 15:53, 54). What does this mean? It means that when we pass from this earthly realm three things will take place. The body will return to the ground from whence it was taken (Genesis 3:19, Job 34:15). The soul will go either to heaven or hell according to the life that was lived here on earth (Ezekiel 3:19-21, 18:4, 20-32, Psalm 9:17, 16:10, Matthew 10:28* 16:26) and all spirits will return to the God that gave it (Ecclesiastes 12:7*, Numbers 16:22, 27:16, Zechariah 12:1, Hebrews 12:9). When we stand before God, then, there will no longer be any flesh that will separate us. We will see God for who he is we will behold him face to face.

In this realm it does not yet appear what we shall be, but we know that when he shall appear (literally) we shall be like him for we shall see him as he is (I John 3:2). Why later? Because that's what faith is. Faith is the substance of things HOPED for and the evidence of things NOT seen (Hebrews 11:1). We live by faith and not by sight and without it (faith) we cannot please God (Hebrews 11:6). Blessed are those who believe and have not seen (John 20:29*, II Corinthians 5:7, I Peter 1:8).

CONCLUSION

My prayer is that someone, through the words in this book, would find the strength to live the life God has called them to. My desire for every reader is to understand that God is not sitting around waiting for us to mess up so he can blot out our names from the book of life. God is in fact a God of longsuffering. However, we must not frustrate the grace of God. It is when we refuse to renew our minds, cease from sin and heed to the call of God that causes our heart to become hardened. This is when we begin to endanger our eternal security. The word of God tells us to warn each other everyday so that none will be deceived by sin and hardened against God. This hardness is considered reprobation, to be void of judgment. When we allow our hearts to become hard we loose the ability to discern good from evil. God said that because he called and ye refused, he stretched out his hand and no man regarded but set at naught all his counsel and would none of his reproof, he (God) said he would laugh when your calamities comes and mock when your fear comes. After your heart has become so hard God will send strong delusion that they will believe a lie, that they all might be damned who believed not the truth but had pleasure in unrighteousness. Please understand God desires that every man, women, boy and girl would come to repentance. He does not take pleasure in the destruction of his people. He stands now waiting for your call. Call unto him and he will answer thee and show thee great and mighty things that you know not of. It will blow your mind the love you will experience after restoration. The word of God says that he, who is forgiven much, loves much. I can honestly say that because God has forgiven me and welcomed me back into his family my love for him has grown tremendously. He could have left me in my mess and let me burn in hell forever but by his mercy he delivered me. I thank God for every thing I've had to go through in this life. Am I proud of every thing? No! But through my own experiences God has revelated his word to me. Because we are in the last days there are several doctrines that are trying to infiltrate the world today stating that once you've confessed Christ as lord your eternal salvation cannot be altered. This is a "spirit of doctrine" that needs to be bound by every born again believer. My prayer is that adequate information and scripture has been given in this book that will show and prove that confession alone in not enough to secure your salvation. Faith, which is hope until manifestation, must be accompanied by works or else it is dead according to GOD'S word.

Often times we as a people like to push blame as to where the fault lies as far as the condition of the world but if we be honest the fault lies with those professing to be in the family of God but are still living after the flesh. We (the sons of God) have been given the power to change our very own world. How can I say that? Well for several reasons do I say it. When God was going to destroy Sodom and Gomorrah, he first consulted with his friend, Abraham. He told him that if he could find "the righteous" then he would spare the cities. Elijiah was a man with like passions as us yet he prayed that it would not rain for three and a half years and the rain held up. God has told us through his word that the prayers of the righteous avail much. Why does the fault lie with us? Because God plainly said that if his people, which are called by his name would humble themselves and pray, and seek his face and turn from their wicked ways then he'd hear from heaven, forgive our sins and heal the land. We can't get the world to turn from their wicked ways because they see that the church has not turned from theirs. Notice God said if his people would turn from their wicked ways, then he'd hear. Sadly to say but every thing in creation is doing what it's supposed to do except the church. Seasons are changing, the sun is shinning, the earth is rotating, sinners are sinning, liars are lying etc. Very little of the requirements that are expected from the church are being met. What are the requirements? To be simple, HOLINESS! Without this attribute no man will see God. Through our holiness we should be reconciling the world unto God. *"Let your light so shine before men that they may see your good works and glorify the father which is in heaven"*. Isn't it funny how the so-called "sinners" know that there is supposed to be a difference between what they do and what a so-called "Christian" does?

God is not slack concerning any of his word and whether we believe it or not, Christ will return one day to receive his people unto himself. Those not prepared for his return will be left behind. Just as in the days of Noah, so shall it be when the Son of man returns, the door will be shut. God is not the only one looking for his offspring; the world is looking, waiting and groaning in expectation for the manifestation of the Sons of God. When Jesus walked this dusty earth, multitudes would flock to him because they knew that he could deliver them. We, the people of God, should be surrounded by multitudes desiring deliverance. Please understand that God does have a remnant of people who are living a life that is pleasing to him and who love him with all of their heart but because the church has allowed so much to go on it's hard, from the view of the world, to tell who's real and who's not. It is important now more than ever for those professing to know God to stand up in might and power. The world is dying at a rapid rate because of the lack of light. We are the light of the world but many of our lights have been dimmed by sin. It's not too late to seek deliverance. Don't buy into the lie that says it doesn't matter how you live as long as you've confessed. Paul said that if an angel came speaking another gospel let him be accursed. God backed him by saying let every man be a lie and God's word be true. Contrary to popular opinion, grace is not a blanket to sin. Grace is the empowerment to live as God has commanded. Hell was not made for you (humanity) but because of the hardness of heart hell hath enlarged itself. If you seek God with your whole heart you will find him. My prayer is that your eyes will be opened, your ears attent and your heart receptive to what the Spirit is saying to the church. *He that endureth unto the end* shall be saved.

CLOSING PRAYERS

NEW CONVERT

If after reading this book you don't want your soul to be found in eternal torment and you have never received Christ into your life you are a new convert, please pray the following prayer:

Lord, I come confessing with my mouth and believing in my heart that you raised Jesus from the dead. I ask you now to come into my life and be my lord. Forgive me God for the sins of my past. I vow now to live for you from this day forth. Congratulations! Your life is just beginning. This the most important thing you will ever do. God loves you and so do I.

BACKSLIDER

If you have had a relationship with God before but for some reason you may have strayed away then you are a backslider. If after reading this book your understanding was enlightened and you want to be placed back in right standing with God, please pray the following prayer:

Lord, I praise you that you are married to the backslider. I come now confessing my sins and you said that if I confess my sins you are faithful and just to forgive me and cleanse me from all unrighteousness. Receive me back into your family I pray. From this day forth I will live for you.

PRAYER OF AGREEMENT

Lord, you see the hearts of these your people. I stand in agreement with them concerning their walk with you. Lord, I loose a Spirit of endurance into their lives that will cause them to finish their race steadfast unto the end. And lord I bind every spirit that is not like you. Use them God for your glory and cause their lives to be living testimonies for you. We claim it and receive it in the precious name of Jesus, Amen

Printed in the United States
32180LVS00007B/46-135

9 781420 849141